MW00654048

RUSSIAN
PROVERBS

Nadezhda (Nadine) Timofeevna Koroton,
Dartmouth's first woman professor

100 Favorites of Professor Nadezhda Timofeevna Koroton

Edited by Vera Politis,
Alan A. Reich and Richard Sheldon

Proverbs translated by Richard Sheldon and Barry Scherr

Dartmouth Triad Associates

ISBN 0-9660504-0-1
Library of Congress Catalog Card No. 97-69418
Published in the United States of America by
Dartmouth Triad Associates
Manufactured in the United States of America

Dartmouth Triad Associates:
Vera Politis
Alan A. Reich
Richard Sheldon

Editors:
Vera Politis
Alan A. Reich
Richard Sheldon

Proverb Illustrators:
Mihail Iakovlev
Svetlana Maximova
Tatiana Pletneva

Proverb Translators:
Barry Scherr
Richard Sheldon

Graphic Designer:
Ron Fraker

Contents

*This book is dedicated
to the memory of
Professor Nadezhda Timofeevna Koroton
by her students and colleagues*

ТЕРПЕ́НИЕ И ТРУД
ВСЁ ПЕРЕТРУТ

Foreword

Francis Bacon's observation that "the genius, wit and spirit of a nation are discovered in its proverbs", is nowhere more true than in Russia, where proverbs grew out of the very roots of the nation's consciousness and its rich folklore. In them we find a store of oral wit and wisdom as immense as the land itself. Linguists and lexicologists worldwide marvel at this priceless treasure and the degree to which proverbs have become an integral part of the Russian people's daily expression.

In my one brief but unforgettable encounter with Professor Koroton, I gained an understanding of the warmth and dedication she gave to her life's purpose of conveying to her students the breadth of her native culture. I can appreciate how she chose to use proverbs so extensively in her teaching, as reflected in this marvelous illustrated collection of her favorites, because they succinctly provide insights into the people and country she had to leave behind. The volume's enthusiastic testimonials of her students attest to her great success both as a teacher and as a loving human being concerned with the future of us all.

I commend the editors for a work well done. They have made accessible to a broader audience a treasury of aphorisms that contains real, often sly wisdom for all of us. Professor Koroton, through this book, continues to help us understand the practical yet often seemingly paradoxical ways that the Russian people think. And so she is contributing still to the wider horizons we now find for interacting more constructively with the people of the land she loved.

James H. Billington, PhD
The Librarian of Congress,
former Professor of Russian History
at Princeton University and
author of *The Icon and the Axe*

Acknowledgements

Russian Proverbs – 100 Favorites of Professor Nadezhda Timofeevna Koroton is the brainchild of Alan A. Reich '52, my mother's and the Russian Civilization Department's first major at Dartmouth College. My mother, Nadine T. Koroton, was deeply attached to Alan and referred to him as her spiritual son.

After mother's death Alan suggested publishing in her memory a book of her favorite Russian proverbs, which she used extensively in her teaching, to be funded by donations from her former students. I thought this was an excellent idea, whereupon Alan got in touch with the Dartmouth Russian Department. Professors Barry Scherr, Department Chairman at that time, and Richard Sheldon, who oversaw the project at Dartmouth during its entire term, enthusiastically endorsed the endeavor. Thus the "Russian Proverbs" project came into being and a team of four was organized to see it through.

It turned out to be a difficult task in the beginning, since the Russian Department had no record of students who took Russian during my mother's tenure at Dartmouth. Fortunately, mother left to me her voluminous notes, writings, correspondence, some class notes, official letters from the college, press articles from the Hanover area and Dartmouth publications. These proved to be vital to our efforts. After searching through this material I compiled a list of some two hundred student names. Further research at Dartmouth's Baker Library enabled me to find a few more names and the Alumni Office provided us with their current addresses.

Alan Reich then contacted Nadine's former students and, through their generous donations, the funds needed for this project were secured. This made the "Russian Proverbs" publication a reality. Regrettably, the student list is incomplete. I estimate that we missed probably more than one-half of her students. To all who were not contacted, and so did not have the opportunity to be part of this project, I offer our sincere apology.

My family is deeply grateful to Alan Reich for initiating this project and for his leadership, which was instrumental in the successful conclusion of this book, and to Professors Richard Sheldon and Barry Scherr for their personal contributions to the book and loyalty to their departed colleague. My thanks also to Maria Georgievna Schalk, Administrative Assistant of the Russian Department, for her excellent work of typing the proverbs in their various renditions. To my friend Mikhail Iakovlev in Moscow, Professor at the Russian Academy of Art, go my thanks for supplying the beautiful proverb illustrations at a reasonable cost. Special thanks to my husband for providing me with his resourceful and practical help throughout this project.

I have always felt very close to my mother's students, having been thoroughly influenced by her warm feelings toward them and by her selfless commitment to their success. Therefore it is with a deep sense of affection and appreciation that I extend my most heartfelt SPASIBO to all her "malchiki", who contributed to this book of tribute to my mother not only financially, but also with their moving reflections and memories of their beloved teacher. It is their book and I know mother would find great pride in it.

VERA PAVLOVNA KOROTON POLITIS

Preface

The life of Nadezhda Timofeevna Koroton spanned the rise and fall of the Soviet Union. Her life and her work were influenced greatly by this dominant event of our century. Midway, she fled the Soviet regime, came to Dartmouth College and devoted herself to preparing her students to interact and cope with – during its remaining years – the nation she had left behind.

Nadine was born in 1901 in the Ukraine, where she received her university degree and taught Russian language and literature. She and her husband, together with their daughter, Vera, survived the Stalin horrors of the 1930's. But when the German Army in World War II advanced into the U.S.S.R., Nadine's husband was arrested and shot by the NKVD, the Soviet Secret Police. Nadine and Vera escaped to Western Europe and for four years lived in dire circumstances in a displaced persons camp in Germany. In 1949, they immigrated to the United States, bringing with them almost no possessions other than a few gold five-ruble pieces.

It was fortuitous that at this time Dartmouth was establishing the Russian Department and its chairman heard of the outstanding Russian teacher who had left her homeland and her profession to escape Soviet Communism. Nadine accepted his offer to teach at the College and arrived in Hanover in the fall of 1950. I had studied beginning Russian, and it didn't take long under Nadine's tutelage before I decided to major in Russian Civilization, the College's first student to do so. Thus began a long friendship that continued until Nadine's death in 1994.

Nadine was beloved by her students. She always welcomed us warmly at One North Park Street, where she gradually saved enough money to furnish her small apartment with a sofa, chair, bookcase, bed and eventually a piano. Her students appreciated not only her outstanding teaching, enriched by her frequent reciting of Russian proverbs, but the borshch and delicious meat pies she would prepare for us. My own Russian language and literature instruction took place as much at One North Park as it did in Dartmouth Hall. Many evenings and Sunday afternoons were spent sitting on the maroon sofa reading Pushkin, Lermontov and Tolstoy aloud. Nadine knew their works by heart. A real taskmaster, she would insist on perfect pronunciation and complete understanding, although I must admit to feigning full comprehension of some of the proverbs that didn't lend themselves to easy translation.

Nadine used proverbs liberally in her classes, because each one captured in a few words so much meaning about Russians and Russian life. She made sure our notebooks were filled with them, along with both their literal and colloquial translations. After her retirement from Dartmouth in 1966, Nadine prepared a list of her favorites, one hundred of which appear in this memorial tribute to her.

Nadine kept us entranced with stories of the unbelievably difficult times she and her family had endured. We came to share her hatred of the Soviet regime, and we became more grateful for our own freedom and way of life. Underlying Nadine's quiet demeanor was a deep belief in God and Orthodox Christianity. She would quote passages from the New Testament as regularly as she would from the works of the Russian 19th century literary giants. She taught us of the spiritual depth of her people.

I am sure many of Nadine's students have wondered, as I have, what path their lives would have taken had they not met her. She inspired many to choose diplomatic or military careers with heavy involvement in Soviet and Russian affairs. Others went into teaching the language or history. Had it not been for Nadine, I certainly would not have chosen Russian Civilization as my Dartmouth major. Nor would I have received a fellowship and a degree in Slavonic Studies at Oxford; lived for a month in a Russian Orthodox monastery in London; interrogated -as an Army officer- Soviet military defectors in Germany; opened -as a State Department official- the U.S. Consulate in Leningrad; negotiated U.S.-Soviet trade agreements; broadcast in Russian on the Voice of America to the people of the U.S.S.R.; or organized a program to send hundreds of wheelchairs donated by paralyzed Americans to needy Russian counterparts. Every day I am reminded of Nadine's profound influence on my own life as I proudly wear, as the centerpiece of my tie clasp, the gold five-ruble piece from her homeland that she presented to me at graduation.

Nadine's admirers and friends extended well beyond her students. As readers of this memorial tribute will see, they included many faculty members, as well as John Sloan Dickey, president of the College throughout her sixteen Dartmouth years. He spoke of Nadine as a powerful addition to the Dartmouth community and frequently inquired about her after her retirement. President Dickey may well have had Professor Koroton in mind when he wrote, in 1964, of "comprehensive awareness" in undergraduate education:

> But I see no way for the college to meet its responsibility for preparing men to "live and learn" comprehensively other than by purposefully and strategically permeating

> the undergraduate experience, in the classroom and outside, with opportunities for the student to become aware of significant human experience that of itself he cannot "take" in the form and depth of a course on the subject. If in this way the college can help the undergraduate to become more comprehensively aware, as in other ways he is made more "professionally" competent, we can count on another unprecedented circumstance of modern life to take up where the college leaves off and "see him through."

In dedicating this memorial tribute to Nadine Koroton, her daughter Vera Politis and I express our grateful appreciation to Professors Richard Sheldon and Barry Scherr of the Dartmouth Russian Department for their tireless and creative efforts. We thank especially Dr. Demetrios Politis, Vera's husband, for his thoughtful advice and caring assistance throughout the project. Most significantly, we thank Nadine's former students, listed at the back, whose donations made the publication possible. They were acknowledged best by Nadine herself when she wrote:

> To teach my students and have contact with them has always been a joy for me. I have always been glad to enter my classroom, to see my students, and to look into their young, good and truthful eyes. They inspired me to do my best, to help them in their progress and to improve my methods of teaching. The students will always be for me my most precious memory.

Nadine would hope, as do Vera and I, that future students at Dartmouth, and indeed everywhere, derive enjoyment and wisdom from *Russian Proverbs – 100 Favorites of Professor Nadezhda Timofeevna Koroton.*

ALAN A. REICH '52

Professor N. T. Koroton's Legacy at Dartmouth

A few women had taught at Dartmouth during the first two centuries of its existence. After the Russian revolution, for example, Dartmouth students clamored for courses in Russian, so the College hired Elizabeth Reynolds Hapgood to meet the demand. In the fall of 1918, eighty-six Dartmouth men promptly enrolled in the course and Dartmouth College became one of the first universities in the United States to offer such courses.

The first woman ever to be admitted to the professorial ranks at Dartmouth, however, was Nadezhda Timofeevna Koroton. Mrs. Koroton and her young daughter had escaped from the Soviet Union as World War II was drawing to a close. After four years in a displaced-persons camp in Munich, she and her daughter had received visas admitting them to the United States, where they arrived in 1949.

In 1950 the Russian Department was looking for a native speaker of Russian who could help the students gain an oral command of the language. Of the various candidates interviewed by the department, Mrs. Koroton made the most favorable impression. She got the job.

Two years later, the Department of Russian Civilization met to reconsider her status. Her performance had been outstanding. The department was afraid that some other university – one with female faculty members! – might hire her away from Dartmouth. Accordingly, the department took the unprecedented step of recommending that she be made a regular member of the faculty.

The meeting took place on March 12, 1952. According to the minutes, Professor von Mohrenschildt "declared that Mrs. Koroton had proved herself to be a first-rate, well-qualified teacher in the three semesters that she has taught Russian here. In view of the high-caliber work she is now doing, von Mohrenschildt felt that the Department of Russian Civilization should do what it can to see that she receive the rank of instructor and be made a full-fledged member of the Dartmouth Faculty." The six members of the department voted unanimously in support of this motion.

In his letter to Dean Donald Morrison urging this unusual appointment, Professor von Mohrenschildt spoke of her "exceptional work," her expertise as a language teacher, and her generosity with her time. He expressed concern that, without some improvement in her situation, she might be tempted to take a position at a coeducational or woman's college. He urged the administration to make an exception in her case. The department's persistence prevailed and Mrs. Koroton was promoted, effective July 1, 1952. She thereby became the first woman in the history of the College to become a regular member of the faculty.

Three years later the administration accepted the department's recommendation that she be promoted once again – this time as Assistant Professor of Russian Civilization. Her work had continued at the same extraordinarily high level and it remained at that level as long as she taught.

Professor Koroton taught at Dartmouth until her retirement at the end of spring term, 1966. It was precisely at that moment that I arrived in Hanover with my wife to begin teaching at Dartmouth as an Assistant Professor. Nadezhda Timofeevna remained in Hanover for a few months before moving to Ann Arbor to join her daughter and granddaughter, so we were able to get together with her from time to time.

Since that time, I have walked by her house on 4 Dorrance Place every day for many years and I never fail to remember the remarkable garden (alas, long gone!) that she cultivated on that small lot and the generations of Dartmouth students whom she nurtured there. I know even from my brief acquaintance with her what a remarkable woman she was. During the thirty years that have passed since she stopped teaching at Dartmouth, her devoted students have continually expressed their affection for her. She has never ceased to be an inspirational presence in the department.

RICHARD SHELDON

Nadine T. Koroton – A Life to Remember

I would like to address this brief introduction about my mother, Professor Emerita Nadine (Nadezhda Timofeevna) Koroton, to the faculty, students and local community of Dartmouth College. It is truly a privilege to be associated with such a fine college. My mother appreciated her association with Dartmouth from the very beginning, not realizing that she was to play an important role in the history of the College.

It is a difficult task to portray in a few pages a radiant, intensely purposeful and interesting person, especially if that person happens to be your mother. From my early childhood on, my relationship with my mother was one of loving loyalty and trust. Her life experiences, before and after communism in Russia, had a lasting influence on the development of my character and world outlook. She enlightened my life with her seasoned wisdom. She lives within me every single day.

In the summer of 1952, at the behest of the Department of Russian Civilization, Nadine Koroton, a displaced person and a political refugee from the Soviet Union, was made a regular member of the faculty. This decision created a historic precedent for Dartmouth College, because in May of 1955 Nadine became the first woman in Dartmouth's history to attain professorial rank in what had been for two centuries an all-male faculty and student body. This honor bestowed upon my mother by one of the finest Ivy League Colleges in America was a great source of pride for her and her family.

In 1955 Nadine also became an American citizen. These two events were for my mother the pinnacle of her American saga. At last she could call herself a free woman and she became a true American patriot, a term which she took very seriously. She knew very well the difference between freedom and slavery and she never hesitated to proclaim her allegiance to her beautiful America. She was a woman of strong convictions, which were molded by her personal tragic encounter with Soviet communism. She would never compromise when it came to facts or truth, no matter how unpleasant they might be.

Fighting communist slavery became a life-long commitment for her. When fellow travelers in the academia tried to intimidate her by warning her to stop talking about marxism and communism, it only strengthened her resolve to expose the horrendous crimes committed by the Soviet regime against their own people. I admired her courage deeply and I followed her example.

Nadine Koroton was an individual of many talents, liked and admired by all who knew her, for her intelligence, warmth, hospitality and profoundly wise philosophy of life. She had a passion for teaching and made a name for herself at Dartmouth as an exceptionally gifted pedagogue, loved and respected by her students. A totally unselfish person, she gave generously of herself and was completely content with whatever came her way from the college. She never complained about anything. She was happy to be in America, a land of freedom and opportunity. She appreciated every day of her life in this country, which provided her with the chance to practice her profession and to have her own home, which gave her freedom of speech and, most importantly, freedom to be herself.

My mother's life was totally absorbed with "her Dartmouth

College" and her "dear American boys." She enjoyed every day of her Dartmouth experience, and when she moved to Ann Arbor to be close to me and my family, I could see how much she missed Dartmouth, her students and the good friends she left behind.

Nadezhda Timofeevna Koroton, née Negeevich, was born to a family of educators. Her father, Timofei Semionovich, was a late 19th century educator. Nadine's mother, Anastasia Pavlovna Leveshko, was a well-educated young lady, skilled in mathematics and a talented painter. She was an enlightened woman for her time.

Both Nadine's parents loved books and subscribed to various literary and political journals, exposing their children to a broad spectrum of cultural and social activities. The family also loved music, and Nadine, taught to play the piano from an early age, became a good pianist. Thus, early in her life Nadine was exposed to the best the Russian intelligentsia could offer.

Nadine's father was the son of a Russian Orthodox priest, Father Semion Negeevich. Fr. Negeevich and his wife had died young while tending to the needs of people who fell ill during a terrible epidemic in the late nineteenth century. The young Timofei and his sister were orphaned at ages ten and eight. They were taken by their maternal uncle, Father Alexei Klepachevsky, to his home in Kremenchug, where they stayed until adulthood. After graduating from university and getting married to Anastasia Leveshko, Timofei Negeevich moved into his ancestral house in Belotserkovka, in the Poltava gubernia (province). There their four children were born, two boys and two girls. Nadine, the second child, was born in February of 1901.

Timofei Semionovich Negeevich inherited the house in Belotserkovka and a small estate in the area, which provided for the family very handsomely. From his parents he had also inherited a strong love for the common people and a desire to improve their lot. He was an "idealist," which in the Russia of those times meant a person striving for social improvement. He built a school in his area with his own funds and taught peasant children himself for 28 years, very much like the famous Russian writer, Leo Tolstoy. He felt it his duty to bring literacy into every house in the village.

Anastasia Pavlovna Leveshko, Nadine's mother, was a "stolbovaya dvorianka," a woman of noble birth and cultured family. She grew up on a large estate, which produced everything from honey to race horses. Her father, a judge and a well-to-do aristocrat and landowner, loved to work on the estate. He especially loved to tend his 500 bee hives and many race horses. Her brothers (Nadine's uncles) were all university graduates, and her sisters (Nadine's aunts) all married into the upper-class cultural and professional gentry. They were a closely knit family, with a long tradition of duty to country, and service in the professions and the military.

It was a great joy for Nadine to visit her maternal grandparents. She stayed there for extended periods of time before she started going to school and later during vacation time. She remembered her Leveshko grandparents with deep love and nostalgia. Theirs was an exotic world of old traditions, children kissing their grandparents' hands and addressing them by the polite form of "Vy" (a sign of deep respect), instead of the familiar "Ty", and making reverences upon meeting them. It was an orderly life with charming peasant customs, beautiful Ukrainian songs and virgin country side, a world forever gone and never to return. Out of the six children Leveshko had, including Nadine's mother

Anastasia, and many grandchildren, Nadine knew only of two who survived the communist holocaust.

The family was Russian Orthodox and worshipped in the cathedral, which was Nadine's grandfather's parish and on the grounds of which Father Simeon (Nadine's grandfather) was buried. Nadine remembered with special fondness the Christmas service and the carolling by children, who carried crosses and stars under the windows of the houses.

Leveshkos and Negeeviches were members of the Russian and Ukrainian cultural elite of their time. So, from early childhood Nadine was exposed to the culture and refinement of the upper class Russian and Ukrainian gentry and the charming Ukrainian peasantry, and developed a strong love for both, her Russian and her Ukrainian background. These sentiments my mother also instilled in me. I was brought up feeling equal love for Russia and Ukraine. Russia and Ukraine merged in our hearts into one and into something special. Local music, local speech and customs evoked strong emotional reactions in both of us.

Nadine experienced the inhumanity and cruelty of the communist state and its ideology early in her life, and learned that communism has no human face. After the Bolshevik revolution, when she was nineteen years old, she, her father and more than 200 other people from her hometown were arrested and marched 60 miles in beastly winter weather to the next town. Upon arrival, exhausted, frozen and hungry, they were packed in schools and churches, together with thousands of other people detained by the Soviet secret police. There they were held for two months in deplorable conditions, interrogated constantly. Some of them disappeared; others were released. Fortunately, she and her father were let go. However, around that time her brother

Vassili was killed by the Bolsheviks. Some time later her family was forced out of their ancestral home and thrown into the street. Her parents were given refuge first by a shoemaker and later by a teacher, who felt sorry for them and took them in. Both her parents died away from their home and their loved ones.

After graduating from gymnasium Nadine enrolled at the university, but was unable to complete her studies because of a new Soviet law that precluded the children of the "undesirable elements" from having a higher education. The "undesirables" were members of the pre-revolutionary intelligentsia, especially those who had been landowners, businessmen, members of the former military, clergy, government officials, police, land-holding farmers, and whomever the communist rulers deemed to be "undesirable." This category of people was defined rather broadly. Therefore, a large number of people were deprived of their civil rights and were banned from voting, even though the voting itself under the communist regime was a farce. The repercussions of this unjust law extended to the children of these socially ostracized victims. Only in 1936, after Stalin's proclamation that "children are not responsible for their parents' background or acts," could Nadine enroll at the university again. Having graduated with honors from two institutes of higher education in the city of Zaporozhie, she was now eminently qualified to do what she loved: teach Russian literature, poetry and language.

In 1923 Nadine married Paul Koroton, an attorney, and had two children with him. The second and surviving one, Vera, the author of this life story, is married to Dr. Demetrios T. Politis and lives in Ann Arbor, Michigan.

Paul Koroton received his education in pre-revolutionary Russia. He was the son of a farmer and former serf in Imperial Russia. Upon graduating from the university, he was commissioned a reserve Officer of the Imperial Army and served with distinction in World War I. Paul came from a family of middle-income Ukrainian farmers. During the forced collectivization and communist-instituted famine, Paul and Nadine saw his parents and family starve to death, together with 7 million other farmers in the Ukraine and millions more in Russia and the rest of the Soviet Union. Nadine was a teacher in a rural area at the time and the horror of the famine and the sight of swollen, starving children, women and men, were imprinted in her mind forever. Witnessing this and other communist atrocities against their own people strengthened her resolve to fight this evil system with all her strength. My mother and I did this in our new country by giving speeches, supporting anticommunist organizations, and helping political prisoners and persecuted Christians in the Soviet Union.

The fact that my father came from a modest background did not save him. He was arrested by the communist secret police five times. Each time was a nightmarish experience for my mother, never knowing whether her husband would come back. I can never forget when at 3 a.m. on a cold March night, secret police, the NKVD (predecessor of KGB), dressed in civilian clothes, took over our small apartment, separated my father from us and started rummaging through everything in our house. Then they took my father with them. I do not know at what age small children start experiencing profound adult-like suffering, but that was when my young heart felt overburdened with agonizing grief. Tormenting questions kept creeping into my inquisitive and untarnished mind about the country I was calling my homeland. It was my first pragmatic encounter with the ugliness of communism. I grew up overnight.

It was a miracle that my father, skeleton-like, returned alive after this arrest. Then came the war and with it his final arrest in 1941. We never saw my father again. This time "They" charged my father under Article 58, which carried the most severe sentence for political prisoners in the Soviet Union, a minimum of 25 years of imprisonment or death. Under this article, the NKVD branded the arrested "an enemy of the people" and "an alien element" deserving to be "liquidated", the communist term for killing people. This they carried out. Thus, a true son of the people, son of a former serf, became an innocent victim of the "people's regime," as the communists referred to their own rule. Paul Koroton, Professor Koroton's beloved husband, together with other political prisoners, perished in the dungeons of the NKVD building, blown up by the secret police before they fled from Zaporozhie during World War II.

My mother, at the age of 40, lost her husband and provider, and I lost my gentle and kind father in a barbaric way that only communists and their secret police henchmen could devise. Victims of communism refer to their secret police and rulers as "bloodsuckers." This is, indeed, their appalling "legacy"!

The agony my mother and I went through left deep and permanent scars in our hearts. We never forgot the bestial cruelty of our personal loss, a loss which was suffered by millions of people during the Soviet terror.

In 1943, determined never again to live under communist tyranny, my brave mother took me and, leaving all our precious but meager possessions in the Soviet Union, left the land of Stalin's vassals. Using every means of transportation available, including very often long days of walking, we made it from the Ukraine to the North Sea coast of Germany. There we were liberated by the British army. We subsequently moved to Munich, in the American occupation zone, where we asked for asylum in the United States. Finally, in October of 1949 my mother and I arrived in New York on a troop transport ship, together with hundreds of other displaced persons.

In the summer of 1950, Dartmouth College was looking for a native Russian to teach in the College's Russian department. Nadine's qualifications (two university diplomas cum laude) made her the obvious choice. In September of 1950, with the help of Professor Harold Washburn and his son John, who was a member of the Department of Russian Civilization, my mother arrived in Hanover, where she finally found the peace and happiness that had eluded her for the past 32 years. In Nadine Koroton, Dartmouth College got more than it had bargained for. It obtained not only an exceptionally gifted teacher, but also an eloquent witness and source of first-hand information about the events in Russia, which had had such a tremendous impact on the lives of millions of people around the world. Nadine became an instant celebrity in the Hanover area.

In spite of the pain and miseries she endured under communism and the loss of her home and many members of her family, including her brother and her husband, Nadine's friends remember her as a lovely lady with a joyful and optimistic outlook on life. The traumatic experiences she went through in life forced her to philosophize about human existence and its meaning. She developed her own interesting ideas and liked to talk on this topic for hours. She would illustrate the beauty of God's earth and God's creations on earth by reciting poems, of which she knew an enormous number. She loved poetry and had a phenomenal memory. Her friends were always amazed how, at the age of eighty, she could recite by heart page after page of poetry. She would compare the human body to "mother earth" and its seasons, its cataclysms. She would quote bits of wisdom from famous writers and add her own to the collection. It was a joy to spend time in her company, in Ann Arbor over a cup of tea, next to her ever-burning fireplace.

When Nadine came to Hanover she was welcomed by her first dear friends, Professor Washburn's family, who had found living accommodations for her close to them on Wheelock Street and introduced her to local people. A year later she moved into a faculty house at One North Park, where she stayed until she had saved enough money to buy her own "capitalistic house," as she liked to refer to it (by early communist standards, home ownership made her a capitalist), at 4 Dorrance Place. Owning her home gave her a sense of security and accomplishment.

Nadine's one-bedroom apartment was unfurnished. The first items she got were a bed and a table. But she was overjoyed that after years of refugee existence in war-torn Europe she finally had an apartment all to herself. Some three days later, a delegation of her students, led by Alan A. Reich, came proudly bearing a present - an attractive floor lamp. They had a hearty laugh with Nadine when they found out that to toast her housewarming they had to sit on the floor around their lamp, which was the only piece of furniture in her living room.

Eventually, this small apartment turned into an elegant and cozy place, thanks to my mother's exquisite taste and her talent for interior decorating. Her artfully and colorfully embroidered pillows and covers, made the place attractive and exotic-looking. Then, at an auction, she bought a piano. She had dreamed of owning one ever since she left her home in Russia. Now she had her music, which meant so much to her. She even taught some of her friends how to play the piano. Gradually she amassed a fabulous collection of music scores and accumulated a very good library, both in Russian and English, as well as in other languages. Now, with her books and her music, she felt complete.

Nadine loved working outdoors in her garden. Her houses in Hanover and later in Ann Arbor, became admired sites for their bountiful and beautiful flowers. She worked in her garden until she was ninety years old. To a large measure, this accounted for her amazing physical stamina into her nineties. All her long life she believed in the golden unity of the intellectual and the physical activities, just as her ancestors did before her.

The passion of her life, however, was teaching and her students, her "American boys." An enthusiastic and inspiring teacher, Prof. Koroton was truly thrilled to be a member of the Dartmouth College faculty. Her excitement was heightened by the sense that she was in America and her long nightmare of life under communism was over for her and her daughter; that she was teaching young Americans about the language, the history and culture of her native land, a country which she loved deeply and which she knew she was destined not to see again. So, besides her natural talents, she put all her heart and soul into it. She was determined that all her students should speak Russian by the end of a one-year course!

There was no limit on the time Nadine would spend to help and motivate her students to learn. Students, sensing her feelings, were inspired and responded in kind. To her enthusiasm to teach they responded with their enthusiasm to learn. Her reward was their progress. On several occasions students petitioned the department to have Prof. Koroton teach courses usually assigned to other people. They developed a great attachment to her, which carried into her retirement, and into her daughter's family, several of them remaining family friends over the years.

Perhaps nothing shows better her dedication to the teaching profession and her commitment to her students than the fact that in her sixteen years of teaching at Dartmouth she did not miss a single class, even when she was sick: "I could not let my students wait and miss a class. Each class is an experience that a student should not miss," she would say. Long after her retirement she continued to remember her "dear American students." Her eyes would light up whenever she talked about them to her daughter's family or to her friends. When I would tease my mother about her obsession with Dartmouth and her students, she would reply, "Those were the best years of my entire adult life."

Professor Koroton enjoyed the company of her students. She found them to be friendly, polite and kind. She frequently organized gatherings in her home, and many times students would stop by on their own. She often entertained not only her students, but also their parents, who wanted to meet her. Sometimes her students would bring their girlfriends from other colleges to introduce them to her. Students also reciprocated her affection, inviting her to the important occasions in their lives, such as weddings, ordination into the priesthood, baptisms, etc.

Nadine also appreciated the gallantry of her male colleagues. The only female member of the faculty, she marched with them at the head of the procession during Commencement. They treated her with politeness and respect, going out of their way to make her feel comfortable. She experienced no male chauvinism. She felt at ease among her colleagues.

During her teaching career at Dartmouth and at Middlebury College summer school, Nadine attended many professional conferences, at which she delivered speeches or read papers. Her academic career was intellectually stimulating and rewarding. Prominent scholars, writers and reporters on Russian affairs, with whom she developed friendly relations, kept in personal contact with her. Among them were Professor Nikolai P. Poltoratzky, Alexandra Tolstoy, Harrison Salisbury, Yuri Krotkov, and her former student, Christopher Wren. Her correspondence with her former students was voluminous. Their letters, preserved in her files, express lasting attachment to their favorite professor.

At Dartmouth, Prof. Koroton had many close friends. She had a special affection for President Dickey and his family. Her relationship with them was cordial and warm. The tragic extended illness of President Dickey and the suffering that it brought to his family was a source of great sorrow to my mother.

Among her colleagues Nadine cherished especially her friendship with Professor of French, Mr. and Mrs. Harold Washburn and their son, Dr. John Washburn, her colleague at the Department of Russian Civilization; Professor of Russian History and Literature, Dimitri S. von Mohrenschildt (Chairman of the Russian Civilization Department in the fifties); Professor of History John C. Adams and his lovely wife Melanie (Professor Adams was the Chair of the Russian Civilization Department in the fifties); Professor of German and Chairman of the German Department, Herbert and Mrs. Sensenig; Registrar and Professor of Mathematics, Mr. and Mrs. Robin Robinson; Professor of French, Mr. and Mrs. Francois Denoeu; Professor of History, Mr. and Mrs. Albert L. Demaree; Editor of the Dartmouth Alumni Magazine, Mr. and Mrs. Charles E. Widmayer; Professor of German Stephan J. Schlossmacher; Professor of Neurosurgery, Dr. and Mrs. Robert C. Fisher; Mrs. Alwine B. Dudley; Professor of Chemistry, Mr. and Mrs. Douglas M. Bowen; Professor of Government and Mrs. Charles McLane; Mr. and Mrs. Jack Matlock; Mr. and Mrs. Peter Jarotski, and many others. Not having my mother with me now, I may have, regrettably, omitted other names of faculty who were close to her.

Nadine also attended regularly the literary gatherings of the Faculty German Club, which met at different houses, including hers. She enjoyed the opportunity to treat her dear friends to her cooking and baking and to entertain them in her cozy and hospitable home. She recalled every one of them with great warmth to the very end of her days.

A strong sense of duty and responsibility guided Nadine's life. She gave generously of her time to community services. She taught community classes in the area and at Lebanon College. Her students there appreciated not only her classes, but also her willingness to share her life story with them. I understood that my mother refused to be paid by the community college, because she wanted her services donated, as a gesture of her gratitude at being part of the local community. I told my mother that to be paid for one's services is the accepted American practice. But she would not hear of it!

Nadine was frequently asked, and never refused, to address various clubs and organizations on the subject of communism in the Soviet Union, a topic on which she was uniquely qualified to speak. She did this out of a deep love for America and in memory of the millions of victims of the Soviet regime. She would categorically refuse any mention of monetary compensation, saying "If I warn my neighbor that his house is on fire, how can I ask and accept payment for this?" That is how my mother was, and it reflected her strong ethical and moral upbringing. I am fortunate to have had her guidance in my life.

Though her own material means were very limited, Nadine never forgot to help those in need by donating, before and after retirement, regularly and generously to religious, philanthropic organizations and groups that she believed were fighting communism. She contributed regularly to the Tolstoy Foundation, an organization that helps refugees (once giving $1,000 for her daughter's life membership) and to the United Negro Fund, acting on her father's belief that access to education should be universal and without prejudice.

Professor Nadine Koroton's life epitomized the quintessentials of character purity and integrity. That is precisely why she excelled in her teaching and radiated so much positive energy in her classes.

And so it was in recognition of her exceptional teaching performance and other multifaceted contributions to the College that Dartmouth took the historic step of elevating her, a woman, to the rank of Assistant Professor. Nadine set another precedent when she retired: she also became the first woman to be granted the rank of Assistant Professor Emerita. This unique double honor befitted a legendary teacher, who challenged and touched the lives of hundreds of Dartmouth students.

Indeed, the greatest tribute to Nadine is the fact that so many of her students remember her and contributed generously to make this publication a reality, some of them more than forty five years since they were in her class! I know of nothing that would have pleased my mother more than the loyalty of her "American boys" and her Russian Department. She loved them dearly and they have not failed her.

– Blessed are those whose memory is cherished. –

VERA PAVLOVNA KOROTON POLITIS

Eternal Memory, Eternal Peace –

Eternal Memory, Eternal Peace –

Eternal peace,
in all its bliss –

Creator's Kingdom –
Gates of Heaven –
received the soul
of my one and only beloved mother. –

Rejoice, sweet angels!
Sing hymns of Glory!
bless souls, anointed
with life immortal!

Resound, church bells,
to still my sorrow,
my earthly tears,
my doubts, my fears!

The throbbing heart
longs day and night
for tender love
at mother's side,
for gentlest kiss,
for kindest smile,
for by-gone years,
her borshch and pies...

With mesmerized spell-bound gaze
to hear her voice near the fireplace,
Age-seasoned wisdom,
stories past,
Russia that was
and Russia last.
The wasted lives
through sharpened knives
of Red catastrophe, ... and lies...
unending, brazen, cynic lies,
of Their utopian Paradise...

My mama's family, her folks,
would live forever in her talks ...
...The perished victims
of a regime she so abhorred,
so bravely fought –

What noble stand,
until her end ! ....

My dearest mother, my closest friend ...

VERA
MARCH 30, 1994

Nadine T. Koroton: Reflections and Memories

From letters to Nadine Koroton, her daughter, A. Reich and Professor R. Sheldon

Melanie Adams (wife of Professor John C. Adams, Chairman of the Russian Civilization Department and Professor of History)

. . ."She was striking in appearance, as well as in personality . . . It was "love at first sight". We all fell in love with Nadine. Her warmth and enthusiasm were contagious . . . She was hospitable in the true Russian tradition . . . generous with her time . . . Her students were very important to her. She appeared to us to be tireless in her efforts to teach her beloved Russian language to "my boys", as she called her students. My husband, too, never missed a chance to consult her on his own difficulties in the language. She was a helpful source of information not found in grammars. Nadine was loving. She was also devout. She had a marvelous courage which people felt. Her really harrowing experiences gave her a strength of character which showed in her expressive eyes . . . Knowing Nadine was a privilege in which my husband and I felt greatly blessed".

Maria Ager (Ann Arbor friend, to Vera, April 1994)

"She was such a beautiful person and always so sweet and hospitable. I have missed her so much. Her spirit, courage and loving kindness will always be there. She lives through you and all that have known and loved her. She was a great human being and gave much of herself and talents to us". . .

John E. Baldwin, Ph.D. '59 (to Professor Sheldon)

"My personal recollections of her classroom presence tend to focus on her great patience with us, her neophyte students, as we attempted to engage a language of considerable difficulty and expressive range. . . The enduring impact of my classes with Madam Koroton relates more than learning some Russian; her capacities for patience, or proper blends of challenge and instruction and encouragement and patience, I have tried to emulate in my own teaching over the years."

Nathan Burkan, Jr. '53 (letter to Alan Reich)

"Although I only took Russian for one year (the verbs destroyed me), I can never forget Nadine Koroton."

Lucien H. Case '54

. . ."There are a couple of other languages I do speak and a few I have failed at: but in no case (save for living in Brazil) did I ever pick even 10% as much "about" the country as I did from Mrs. Koroton . . . I have been inculcated with a very deep and very true feeling for the country, the people and the customs.". . .

James M. Culberson, Jr. '51 (to NTK, June 16, 1966)

"It was with amazement and sadness that I read of your retirement as Assistant Professor of Russian Language and Literature at the College. I was sad that many future students at Dartmouth will not have the opportunity to learn and study under you. I know that I speak for all of your students when I tell you how much I enjoyed studying under you and visiting with you in your home" . . .

Rev. Richard Ellis '52

"Whenever I think of Mrs. Koroton these days, I see a woman in her late forties with a magnificent Slavic face, hair pulled back in a bun, and an expression of joy and confidence on her face. All of us students were very fond of her and she treated us as though we were her sons. For some of us she was doubtlessly a "mother away from home." As a woman she added something very special to all male faculty. In spite of the pain and suffering she had suffered as a Soviet citizen, she was always cheerful with the most radiant smile you could imagine. She had a big, big heart and took great interest in all of her students. She often used to entertain us at her home, . . . and there she always showed that extraordinary hospitality characteristic of the Russian people . . . When I was ordained a deacon in the Episcopal Church much to my amazement one of the people who drove down with Bishop MacBurney was Mrs. Koroton . . . She was deeply moved by the ordination because it was one of her boys who was being ordained and because she possessed that wonderful faith found in Orthodox Christians. There aren't many faculty members who would have so honored one of their students, and I shall remember her kindness and thoughtfulness to my dying day . . . I stopped in Ann Arbor to see Vera and to visit Nadezhda Timofeevna's grave. I knew how much it would mean to Nadezhda Timofeevna if one of her students came to her final resting place. Tsarstvo yei nebesnoe!"

Paul Floyd,

"I miss your class very much. It was one of the most enjoyable courses I ever had."

Robert S. Hagen '69

"The idea of Professor Koroton's favorite proverbs is splendid . . . I remember her with much affection, as I am sure do all her "mal'chiki", as she called us. Of course, it was a memorable event to be invited to her house for tea, as was her custom every term, but I remember even more vividly one snowy morning in the winter of 1965-66, as I was heading to Dartmouth Hall for her eight o'clock class, I met her on the icy sidewalk and she took my arm as we walked up the hill. It was a gesture which made an enormous impression on a young freshman, one I have never forgotten.". . .

Thomas Ilfeld (to NTK, January 24, 1964)

"I hope that it is not improper for a pupil to write to his teacher. I want you to know, though, how much I enjoyed studying under you. A thousand words of thanks cannot surpass my own feelings. You are such a wonderful teacher . . . I am preoccupied by pre-medical courses, but I will never forget what you have taught me – yes, I remember!". . .

Arthur E. Jensen, Dean of the Faculty – January 18, 1957 letter to NTK

. . ."while I am writing to you, I should like to say that all reports that have come to me about your teaching have been excellent. We shall miss you that semester and will be delighted when you return to us." (sabbatical leave)

Professor Reuben L. Kahn (Kahn test developer), University of Michigan

. . ."You gave a wonderful talk before the Thursday-luncheon group. At the end of the talk you were surrounded by so many of the members that I did not want to disturb the conversation . . . Meanwhile, last Thursday one of the members got up and said that I deserve a special thanks . . . because I brought Professor Koroton to the previous meeting. So you can see what a wonderful impression you left with the group! My wife joins me in sending best wishes to you and yours."

Colman W. Kraft '53 (to Vera Koroton Politis)

. . ."I begin to recollect . . . The face of the most humane woman I have encountered readily returned. The unforgettable word "molodets" still echoes in ears grown older, ears that now fully understand her "starost-nie radost'". . . Then came Alan's letter to JOF which included the excerpt from your mother's paper. The excerpt speaks for itself . . . and the rest is the inner feelings we are offered by those who shape us: dusha-skromnost, – your mother."

David Lagomarsino, Associate Dean of the Faculty, Dartmouth College
(January 23, 1997, letter to Vera Koroton Politis)

. . ."It is wonderful to see the depth of affection for your mother expressed in the many gifts from her former students that have come in to honor her memory. She was clearly an extraordinary mentor."

Caleb Loring III '66

. . ."Nadezhda was a lovely lady and helped me learn to

appreciate the Russian language and culture in a way that still impacts me today."

Professor Charles B. McLane, former Chairman, Russian Civilization Department (letter to Vera Koroton Politis)

"For sixteen years in the 1950s and 1960s Nadezhda Timofeeva Koroton was the lynch pin of Russian language instruction at Dartmouth. There werc times – as in the crush of aspiring new linguists after sputnik (1957) – when others in the Department helped out, but it was Nadezhda who trained a generation of Dartmouth students and in the process did much to shape their character. Coming from harrowing and tragic scenes in wartime Ukraine, she showed a resilience and fortitude admired by all who knew her. Her dedication to her teaching was transfixing." . . .

Donald H. Morrison, Dean of the Faculty – May 4, 1955 letter to NTK

"I would like to add my personal gratitude for the fine and continuing contribution which the official college has recognized by voting you the status of Assistant Professor. . ."

Howard N. Newman '56

"I recall Mrs. Koroton with great affection. She was a wonderful teacher and a kind and generous person."

Emery L. Pierson '53

"Nadezhda Timofeevna was a profound force and influence in my life. She was responsible for a kind of intellectual and spiritual awakening that transformed my entire experience in Hanover". . .

Professor Robin Robinson (letter to Vera Koroton Politis)

"My own warm friendship with Nadine Koroton came about from our common membership in a German reading group, the Deutsches Kraenzchen, which had a nearly continuous existence from 1926 to 1992 . . . We met monthly at the homes of the members . . . Our periodic meetings at Mrs. Koroton's self-styled "capitalistic house" were always warmly anticipated, for the warm hospitality of our hostess, for the delicious refreshments, usually with a Russian or German motive, and for the cordial friendships which developed as time progressed . . . Mrs. Koroton became a good friend of my whole family . . . She was one of our warmest friends over her years in America."

Chris Rood '54 (to NTK)

. . ."Your talk was, without a doubt, one of the most impressive I have ever heard. I believe that it was the first time any of us had gotten a true look at the situation as it is in reality within Russia . . . I consider it my privilege to have met and heard so gracious and charming a woman as yourself."

Angus Russell '52

"What an inspirational teacher she was! Full of dignity, warmth, humor and academic demands. It did not come out until much later what kind of a life she had had in the Soviet Union and Germany. That knowledge just served to make her all the more impressive. She maintained her dignity even during the summer of 1952 when we were at the Middlebury summer school together, along with a number of other summer faculty and students who were clearly communist "fellow travelers", to her intense dismay. I thank her often as I continue with my studies of the Russian language, 45 years later, just for the fun of it and for the exercise of my brain in a way completely unrelated to my profession. But for her, I'm sure I wouldn't be doing it."

Harrison E. Salisbury (The New York Times), March 25, 1955 (letter to NTK)

"I just want to express my appreciation for the very, very pleasant hour spent with you on the Dartmouth campus. I do not have to tell you how rare and real a privilege it is to meet with one like yourself who not only comes from Russia but who has the spirit and the soul of her motherland so much in her heart.". . .

Harrison E. Salisbury, April 22, 1955 (letter to NTK)

. . ."I was thrilled to get your letter last night and to learn that in a few days now you will be an American citizen. Let me be among the first to congratulate you and may you be as happy in your new citizenship, as you were sad in the old. . ."

L. Vincent Sawyer, Jr. '59 (letter to Professor Sheldon)

"Professor Koroton was very special to those of us of US origin, because she was so grateful for the freedom she found in our country. She was a very caring person who gave unreservedly of herself to her students. I'm pleased to help with others of her students in this project to continue her memory and recognize her gifts to Dartmouth".

Dr. Oleg Schidlowsky (a friend)

"Nadezhda Timofeevna loved the country of her birth deeply and passionately and that is why she was uncompromising towards communism. She taught many how to understand and cherish the traditions of the rich Russian culture. My family will never forget her warmth and her generosity. The image of Nadezhda Timofeevna will forever remain in our hearts."

George F. Sherman '52 (letter to Professor Sheldon)
"I am honored to donate to the Memorial Project for Nadezhda Timofeevna Koroton. I cannot think of a more apt memorial than the illustrated collection of 100 Russian proverbs culled from her papers. I shall always remember Nadezhda Timofeevna for her deep humanity and loving patience in first introducing me to the beauty of the Russian language and the wondrous mystery of her homeland. As with so many of my generation at Dartmouth, her sensitive teaching changed the course of my life. Thank you, your colleagues and especially her daughter, Vera, for organizing this remembrance."

Mark I. Starr, Esq. '55 (letter to Professor Sheldon)
. . . "But there was far more to my Koroton experience than learning a language. Nadine Koroton was and to me will always be a very special person. I shall never forget her . . . She was a warm, natural, friendly and happy person, as well as worldly and intellectually wise. Her counsel extended beyond teaching Russian, was always well thought out and practical. I recall it was always offered with a smile. It is over forty years since my Dartmouth graduation. I have clear memories only of two of my professors, Arthur Wilson and Nadine Koroton."

William Mills Todd III '66 (letter to Alan Reich)
"As I read over your list of proverbs, I can close my eyes and hear Professor Koroton's voice . . . She was,

indeed, a "wonderful person and teacher", and your article movingly captures the rigorous, tireless, and inspiring qualities of her teaching". . .

Dr. John Nelson Washburn, Esq. '45 (a colleague)
"Nadezhda Timofeevna was always a source of wisdom, good advice mixed with realism". . . "I like to think of Nadezhda Timofeevna as a doer of good deeds while enlightening Dartmouth College students and the entire Hanover community.". . .

Henry Werner '34, father of NTK's student Peter Werner '68 (letter to NTK)
"Thank you for a very gratifying and inspiring class . . . my opportunity to attend one because of my son Peter. I recall my classes in Dartmouth Hall . . . with professors B. and M. in Latin and Classical Civilization and being inspired for the rest of my life. Let me say that your warmth and kindness towards your students, including my son, made me feel that his education today is just as rewarding . . . Let me repeat my gratitude for teachers like you and God bless you."

Daniel J. Whitaker '62 (in a letter to NTK)
. . ."Words cannot really express the appreciation I have for your generous hospitality this afternoon. The opportunity to discuss problems with a professor is, I feel, all too often missed at college. I really appreciate your interest in my work and your generosity."

David A. Wilbur '64
"I will be eternally grateful for all your help that you offered me in my efforts to master the Russian language!"

Charles J. Zimmerman, Dartmouth Trustee (to NTK, June 16, 1966)

"Dear Professor Koroton: At the Trustees' meeting last weekend I learned that you are planning to retire from the academic ranks. Because I could not remain over in Hanover for Commencement this year and thus did not have an opportunity to extend my good wishes to you personally, I do so now by letter. At the same time I want to express my thanks to you for the distinguished service you have rendered over the years to the College, to its students, and to the cause of higher education. Certainly you must feel a great deal of satisfaction in the knowledge that yours has been a most important role in the development of many young men". . .

AEGIS PUBLICATIONS, John E. Galt, Faculty Editor - September 27, 1965

"Dear Professor Koroton: In continuing the tradition of honoring excellence in the faculty of Dartmouth, the 1966 AEGIS has selected you to receive special coverage in this year's volume". . .

THE DARTMOUTH - Saturday, May 21, 1955

Hanover - "I have my country now. I can sleep quietly and no one will arrest me," beamed Nadezhda T. Koroton of the Russian Department, the only female member of the faculty to reach professional rank". . .

VALLEY NEWS - June 18, 1955

Hanover - A Hanover woman who escaped the terror of Soviet rule recently passed two important milestones in her life. She became the first woman in Dartmouth College's 186 years to achieve professorial rank and she received what to her is perhaps more valued recognition, citizenship in the United States of America[a]. Mrs. Nadezhda T. Koroton was named by the Board of Trustees as Assistant Professor of Russian Civilization, five years after she came to teach in the College's growing Russian Department. Search of registrar office records fails to reveal any woman who has ever held a Dartmouth faculty post of professorial rank. . .

DARTMOUTH COLLEGE
HANOVER, N.H.

THE PRESIDENT

June 13, 1966

Dear Professor Koroton:

It gives me great pleasure to inform you that at their meeting on June 11 the Board of Trustees voted to elect you Assistant Professor of Russian Language and Literature, Emeritus, in recognition of your long and devoted service to the College.

I know full well that my words cannot add anything to the satisfactions you have known in your daily work but both for myself personally and for all the members of the Dartmouth family whom you have served, I want to record this abiding word of great and genuine appreciation.

I hope that the years ahead may provide frequent opportunities for us to see each other and to continue our association in the fellowship of the College and this community.

With all best wishes.

Sincerely,

Professor Nadezhda T. Koroton
4 Dorrance Place
Hanover, New Hampshire

Dartmouth College Archives

If someone had told me in Soviet Russia, where I lived and taught until 1944, that I would live, teach and after 16 years of teaching retire in the U.S.A., I would never have believed it. But the charity of God is boundless. After 27 years of life under communism in Soviet Russia, a life of want, of oppression, of hard irreparable losses and fear, the iron curtain was brought down by the war. I, with my only daughter and thousands of others from our city escaped. Hoping only for God's help, having no money, no friends in Europe, with the war raging around, but strongly feeling in our hearts "better to be dead than under the Red", we crossed Poland and Germany by all kinds of transportation, very often by foot.

The charity of God is boundless

Here I am, living and working in the greatest country of the world, and here I belong. I am living among the kindest and happiest people of the world, and I thank them for this. But I have a feeling of guilt, because I have not told them more often about the enemy, which wants to destroy their way of life. Having more contact with my students, meeting them in my home and the office, I have always gladly answered all their questions about Soviet Russia and life under communism.

Dartmouth College Archives

To teach my students and to have contact with them has always been a joy for me. I have always been glad to enter my classroom, to see my students, and to look into their young, good and truthful eyes. They inspired me to do my best, to help them in their progress and to improve my methods of teaching. The students will always be for me my most precious memory.

May God, our Lord, help them to be happy and never to forget that it was their good fortune to be born in the great country, the United States of America.

May God help them to save the American traditions through the preservation of patriotism to their country.

NADINE KOROTON, 1967
(from her files)

Dartmouth College Archives

Faculty of Russian Civilization, 1959
From left to right: Basil Milovsoroff, Assistant Professor of Russian Civilization; Charles B. McLane, Professor of Russian Civilization and Government; Nadezhda T. Koroton, Assistant Professor of Russian Civilization; Robert E. Huke, Professor of Russian Civilization and Geography; John C. Adams, Professor of Russian Civilization and History; Earl T. Sikes, Professor of Russian Civilization and Economics; H. Gordon Skilling, Professor of Russian Civilization and Government; Dimitri von Mohrenschildt, Professor of Russian Civilization and History; Elmer Harp, Professor of Russian Civilization and Anthropology.

Russian Club, 1951–52
From left to right, Standing: Mr. Omelchenko (guest); Richard Armstrong; John Huck; Richard Ellis; Ed Parsons; Nate Burkan; Richard Morse; Peter Jarotski, Instructor; Ed Klima. *Sitting:* Angus Russell; Mrs. Dudley (guest); Katia Jarotski; Sherman Horton; Professor Koroton; John Washburn, Instructor; Alan Reich.

Dartmouth College Archives

Faculty of Russian Civilization, 1952
From left to right: Rene Fuelop-Miller, Earl T. Sikes, Dimitri von Mohrenschildt, John C. Adams, Nadezhda T. Koroton, Lloyd Trevor, John Washburn.

Dartmouth College Archives

Russian Club, 1957
First row: Phil Schmitter, Richard Jacob, Prof. Koroton, Jim Bryant, Ken Platnick.
Second row: Marvin Bender, Sam Swansen, Erwin Butler, Paul Oltman, Pat Morris.

Under the faculty-supervision of Professor Koroton and the patronage of Professor Adams, Chairman of the Russian Civilization Department, the Russian Club enjoyed an interesting and successful year of activities. Composed of students taking Russian courses in the College, the Russian Club also consists of other interested members of the student body. In order to better acquaint the members with Russian culture and the Russiin people, the Club sponsored lectures by members of the Dartmouth faculty as well as guest speakers. Forums, movies, and conversations and song meetings rounded out a program which covered topics of an economic, historical, literary, philological, and sociological nature. Relations were maintained with other Russian Clubs in the New England area, notably Vassar and Smith, and tentative plans for joint activities were discussed.

—*AEGIS* –1957

Dartmouth College Archives

Professor N.T. Koroton in class, 1959

Professor N.T. Koroton with her daughter, Vera, in her house at 4 Dorrance Place, Hanover, 1962.

The Russian Proverb

A few languages may be richer in proverbs than Russian, but certainly not many. Vladimir Dahl, the great 19th-century Russian ethnographer, dialectician and writer, gathered over 30,000 entries for his collection of 1862 entitled *Proverbs of the Russian People*. While not every item he included would be classified by modern scholars as a proverb, the great majority do fit the definition, and subsequent collections have added many thousands more to the known repertoire.

Just what are proverbs? Essentially, they are brief aphorisms that are concerned with various aspects of everyday life and which have entered into the common store of the popular language. Although sometimes of literary origin, they are often said to express "folk wisdom" about a wide range of topics. They may remark on temporal, spatial or causal relationships between various phenomena (Нет дыма без огня / *Where there's smoke, there's fire*), and they are often concerned with human existence (Старость - не радость / *Old age is no joy*), with family relationships (В семье не без урода / *There's a black sheep in every family*), the relationship of the individual and society (Семеро одного не ждут / *The majority rules*), and admonitions for wise or proper behavior (Меньше говори, больше делай / *Actions speak louder than words*).

While some proverbs contain a single element (Правда глаза колет / *The truth hurts*), it is far more common to find proverbs in which two items, whether concrete or abstract, are brought together in some fashion (Правда дороже золота

/ *One truth is worth a thousand lies*). Sometimes, as in this example, two things are being compared, with one better (or stronger or more valuable, etc.) than the other. At other times the point lies in the very contrast: Глупый осудит, а умный рассудит / *A fool will condemn, but a wise man will ponder*. Comparison, therefore, is one of the most frequent devices found in proverbs, and it is used to express the very essence of a judgment or observation. But the two segments do not necessarily involve a juxtaposition. The second element may in some way modify or expand upon the first: Нет худа без добра / *Every cloud has a silver lining*. Very often one part defines the other, as in Повторенье - мать ученья / *Repetition is the mother of learning*. And numerous proverbs are based on an "if...then" construction, though nearly always the Russian will omit the word for "if" and instead use either an imperative construction (Век учись, а дураком умрёшь / literally: *Study for a century, you'll still die a fool*) or an infinitive (Волков бояться - в лес не ходить / *If you're afraid of wolves don't go into the forest*).

As A. G. Grigorian has remarked, proverbs can be said to lie on the boundary between words and text. That is, they can be drawn upon much as individual words are, and in that sense are both generalized and repeatable. On the other hand, they also exhibit features that are normally ascribed to texts: they are created to describe specific phenomena and have an integral structure; in this regard they are concrete and unique. Therefore, proverbs are simultaneously the means for creating texts (similar in function to words) and meaningful texts in their own right. Another major figure from the 19th century, the philologist Alexander Potebnia, put it in a slightly different way, seeing proverbs as representing a concentration of thought. They thus resemble poetry, both in their abstraction and in their highly structured, condensed manner of expression.

Potebnia also saw proverbs as frequently deriving from fables. Very often a portion of a fable, especially those lines containing the moral, will enter the language as a proverb; in these cases the meaning of the proverb may be clear only because the original fable is a part of the common linguistic tradition. Such is the case, for example, with many of the phrases from the greatest of the Russian fabulists, Ivan Krylov, which are a part of nearly every Russian's repertoire but are often meaningless to students of Russian. What, for instance, is one to make of Да только воз и ныне там / *But the cart is still there*? For the proverb to be meaningful, one has to know Krylov's fable, "The Swan, the Pike, and the Crab," about three creatures, each attempting to pull a cart in a different direction and getting nowhere.

While most often phrases simply grow out of various folk expressions and over a period of time become sufficiently widely used to be termed "proverbial," literary proverbs, such as those derived from Krylov's fables, are hardly uncommon. And very often they are far less enigmatic than Да только воз и ныне там; thus even someone who has never heard of Krylov's fable "The Cuckoo and the Rooster" can probably guess the meaning of Кукушка хвалит петуха за то, что хвалит он кукушку / *The cuckoo praises the rooster because the rooster praises the cuckoo* (i.e., *You scratch my back and I'll scratch yours*). If Krylov probably gave more proverbs to Russian than any other writer, then the playwright Alexander Griboedov was not far behind. His one major work, *Woe from Wit* (*Горе от ума*), introduced dozens of phrases into the Russian language. As with Krylov, some depend on a knowledge of the work, but others are more readily obvious: Злые языки страшнее пистолета/ literally: *Malicious tongues are more fearsome than a revolver*. Sometimes the source can be both folk and literary: Gogol attributes Нечего на зеркало пенять, коли рожа крива/ *Don't blame the mirror if your mug is crooked* to a folk saying, but no doubt those who are familiar with it these days recall it because Gogol himself used the phrase as the epigraph for his play *The Inspector General (Ревизор)*. Indeed, the relationship between literature and proverbs is frequently complex. Many people know Жизнь прожить - не поле перейти / literally: *To live one's life is not like crossing a field* because it appears as the final line of Boris Pasternak's famous poem on "Hamlet." Or Где любовь, там и Бог / *Where love is, God is also* owes its familiarity in part to its use by Tolstoy as the title for one of his well known tales.

In addition to serving as titles or quotations, proverbs often play an imaginative role within literary works. Thus when Dostoevsky wants to show that Pyotr Verkhovensky, the evil conspirator in his novel *The Devils*, has no real understanding of the Russian people, he has him say это лишь ягодки/ *these are just the berries*. But the saying is Это только цветочки, а ягодки ещё впереди. / literally: *These are just the blossoms – the berries are yet to come* (i.e., *The worst is yet to come*). In other words, had Pyotr Verkhovensky really remembered or comprehended the saying correctly, he would have said "these are just the blossoms." Pyotr's father, Stepan, is presented by Dostoevsky as a person who, while kindhearted and well-intentioned, is too strongly influenced by Western ideas and thus separated from a true connection with Russia. As a sign of this quality, the narrator mentions that Stepan would sometimes translate Russian proverbs into French in a most absurd way – i.e., as though making fun of the popular heritage. In *The Brothers Karamazov*, when Dostoevsky wants to indicate the pedantic nature of a German doctor, he has him remark during his testimony at a trial: "But the Russian proverb says, 'If a person has a mind that's good, but if another intelligent person visits him, then that would be still better, for then there will be two minds, and not just one'." The prosecutor impatiently interrupts with the actual proverb: Ум хорошо, а два - лучше / *Two minds are better than one.* Dostoevsky may use proverbs in a straightforward fashion to characterize a figure, but the manner in which he plays with proverbs, as in the cases here, is especially remarkable. He or his characters may confuse them, turn them inside out, reinterpret them, or use them as the source of puns: Англии бояться, никуда не ходить / *If you are afraid of England. you can't go anywhere* (cf. Волков бояться - в лес не ходить / *If you're afraid of wolves don't go into the forest* [figuratively: *If you can't stand the heat, stay out of the kitchen*). In the hands of a skilled author like Dostoevsky, proverbs become a highly useful tool for the practice of the writer's art.

Many of the proverbs popular in Russia today came into the language from elsewhere. Бог дал, Бог и взял / *The Lord giveth and the Lord taketh away* comes from the Book of Job, while Не мечи бисер перед свиньями / *Don't cast pearls before swine* goes back to the Gospel of Matthew. Молчание - знак согласия / *Silence gives consent* is derived from a line in Sophocles via an epistle by Pope Boniface VIII. Sometimes a foreign saying appears to have given birth to a Russian variant. Thus the Latin *De gustibus non disputandum* appears in Russian literally as О вкусах не спорят, but one can also find the much more Russian sounding На вкус и цвет товарища нет. And then there are those translations which did not go entirely smoothly. The French word "assiette" can refer to a stable position or setting, which gave rise to the expression "Il n'est pas dans son assiette" (*He's not in his usual mood* or *He's out of sorts*). However, "assiette" can also mean plate, and thus the saying was translated into Russian as Он не в своей тарелке / literally: *He's not in his plate*, but in fact used figuratively in Russian with the same meaning as the original French.

And of course it is important to note that the supply of proverbs is never constant: Some proverbs fall into disuse and eventually oblivion (though few disappear entirely; while not all the over 30,000 entries in Dahl are in common use anymore, nearly all would still be readily comprehensible to the contemporary speaker). Meanwhile, others are constantly coming into the language, often reflecting phenomena that were unknown a century ago but many also dealing with age-old aspects of everyday life. Perhaps in modern times literary sources, the press, and even popular culture account for an increasingly large percentage of the new proverbs, but many are still distillations of folk wisdom that gain wide currency.

Whether new or old, proverbs frequently exhibit features of meter, rhythm, rhyme, and sound harmony – the essential features of poetry. This is not true of every proverb (cf. Не в деньгах счастье / *Money can't buy happiness*), but, thanks in measure to the two-part structure of many proverbs most will at least reveal some aspect of structuring. A relatively basic form consists of a simple parallelism, with perhaps the repetition of a word or a root: Ученье - свет, а неученье - тьма / *Learning is light; ignorance is darkness*. More often, there is at least some attempt at sound harmony among the words, as in Жизнь прожить - не поле перейти / *Life is not a bowl of cherries.* Here there is no actual rhyme, but the parallelism between the two halves of the proverb, the alliteration that marks three of the key words, the repetition of 'ж' in the first two words, and the carry over of three consonant sounds from the last word in the first half to the last word in the second, all create the sense of a finely molded whole.

Both of the last two examples illustrate another common feature of proverbs, the existence of two strong stresses in each of the two segments. Sometimes the stresses will be so situated that a proverb will follow one of the main metrical patterns of Russian verse. Лу́чше хле́б с водою, чем пиро́г с бедо́ю / literally: *Bread with water is better than pie with trouble.* Here the stress on the first word is probably meant to be weak, though however it is interpreted both halves of the proverb exhibit perfect trochaic trimeter patterns. But if we look at Жи́знь прожи́ть - не по́ле перейти́ again, we see that the first part seems to be in trochaic dimeter, the second part in iambic trimeter. This mixing of different metrical types, while breaking with the norms of Russian literary verse (at least until recent times, when such experimentation does occur now and again), constitutes a quite common phenomenon in Russian folk poetry.

The most obvious formal feature of Russian proverbs, though, is rhyme. Не имей сто рублей, а имей сто друзей / literally: *Don't have 100 rubles – have 100 friends.* Here the rhyme is strengthened by the identity of words leading up to the rhyme pair, and this kind of "enrichment" (the use of supplemental sounds to strengthen the sensation of rhyme) is particularly common in folk verse. End rhyme serves the important function of delineating the borders of each segment and enables the listener to perceive the poetic structure of the whole more easily. Also possible are double rhymes, of the sort: Дру́жба - дру́жбой, а слу́жба слу́жбой / literally: *Friendship is friendship, but duty is duty*. Here the first words of each section rhyme, as do the last words. So-called "internal rhyme" (rhyme involving words not at the ends of a line or unit) is found frequently in folk verse. In this example it is used to complement the end rhyme, but sometimes it may replace end rhyme in whole or in part; note Без труда́ не вы́тянешь и ры́бы из пруда́ / *A cat in gloves catches no mice*, where the rhyme is between the end word of the second part and the initial main word (труда) rather than the last in the first part. Rhyme in proverbs is particularly rich and varied, and some researchers believe that among the various genres of folk verse proverbs were the first to exhibit rhyme.

Thus the formal elements that give proverbs their vitality repay close examination, but it is equally worthwhile to sit back and savor proverbs for pure pleasure. Dahl groups his proverbs by topic and manages to fill a dozen pages just under the category of "language," to say nothing of others on that subject scattered under different headings. For that matter the main grouping titled "intelligence" takes up 16 pages, and the cluster of categories devoted to "sorrow" occupies over 20 pages (the sheer numbers alone may offer some insight into Russian culture and the Russian mind). One learns from Dahl that not only does *Truth stab the eyes* (Правда глаза колет), but it also *stings the ears* (Правда уши дерет); if *Truth is dearer than gold* (Правда дороже золота); it is also *brighter than the sun* (Правда светлее солнца). As the proverb says, На всякое слово есть пословица / *For every word there's a proverb*.

So, once you have read and enjoyed this collection of Professor Koroton's favorite proverbs, go on to look for the many others that enrich the language and that reveal much about the Russian way of life. A knowledge of Russian proverbs will prove invaluable when trying to express your own ideas; coming up with precisely the right proverb is much like coming up with precisely the right word, for *a good proverb gets to the point* (Добрая пословица не в бровь, а прямо в глаз / literally: *A good proverb does not land on the brow but directly into the eye*).

The information in the above essay is based on the following sources:

Dahl', V. I. *Poslovitsy russkogo naroda* [Proverbs of the Russian people]. Moscow: GIKhL, 1957. A corrected reprint of the 1862 edition.

Grigor'ian, A. G. "Poslovitsa v zerkale poslovitsy" [The proverb in the mirror of the proverb]. In *Slavianskoe i balkanskoe iazykoznanie: Struktura malykh fol'klornykh tekstov*. Ed. S. M. Tolstaia and T. V. Tsiv'ian. Moscow: Nauka, 1993. pp. 216–27.

Lazutin, S. G. *Poetika russkogo fol'klora* [The poetics of Russian folklore]. Moscow: Vysshaia shkola, 1989.

Potebnia, A. A. "Iz lektsii po teorii slovesnosti" [From lectures on the theory of literature; originally published in 1894], rpt. in his *Estetika i poetika*. Moscow: Iskusstvo, 1976.

Shtokmar, M. P. "Stikhotvornaia forma russkikh poslovits, pogovorok, zagadok, pribautok" [The verse form of Russian proverbs, sayings, riddles and catch phrases]. *Zvezda vostoka*, 1965, no. 11, pp. 149–63.

Sokolov, Iu. M. *Russkii fol'klor*. Moscow: Uchpedgiz, 1938.

Vladimirtsev, V. P. "F. M. Dostoevskii i narodnaia poslovitsa" [Dostoevsky and the popular proverb]. *Russkaia rech'*, 1996, no. 5, pp. 102–105.

Barry P. Scherr

Proverbs

with literal translation (**in bold font**)
and an English equivalent (*in italic*).

Stresses are indicated for the
convenience of the reader.

Proverbs translated by Richard Sheldon and Barry Scherr

*Illustrations by Mihail Iakovlev,
Svetlana Maximova and Tatiana Pletneva*

I

БА́СНЯМИ СЫТ НЕ БУ́ДЕШЬ.

You won't get full with fables.

Fine words butter no parsnips.

2

БЕЗ ТРУДА́ НЕ ВЫ́ТЯНЕШЬ И РЫ́БКИ ИЗ ПРУДА́.

Without effort you can't even drag a small fish out of a pond.

A cat in gloves catches no mice.

3

БЫ́ЛО, ДА СПЛЫ́ЛО.

It just came and went.

Here today, gone tomorrow.

4

ВЕК УЧИ́СЬ, А ДУРАКО́М УМРЁШЬ.

If you study for a century, you'll still die a fool.

Learning does not a wise man make.

5

ВЗЯ́ЛСЯ ЗА ГУ́Ж, НЕ ГОВОРИ́, ЧТО НЕ ДЮ́Ж.

Once you've committed yourself to (move) cart, don't say you are not up to it.

In for a penny, in for a pound.

6

ВОЛКО́В БОЯ́ТЬСЯ - В ЛЕС НЕ ХОДИ́ТЬ.

If you're afraid of wolves, don't go into the forest.

If you can't stand the heat, stay out of the kitchen.

7

В СЕМЬЕ́ НЕ БЕЗ У́РОДА.

There's no family without a freak.

There's a black sheep in every family.

8

ВСЯК ЧЕЛОВЕ́К СВОЕГО́ СЧА́СТЬЯ КУЗНЕ́Ц.

Each person is the forger of his own happiness.

One is the master of his own fate.

9

ВСЯ́КОЕ НАЧА́ЛО ТРУ́ДНО.

Every beginning is hard.

If at first you don't succeed, try, try again.

10

В ТИ́ХОМ О́МУТЕ ЧЕ́РТИ ВО́ДЯТСЯ.

In a quiet pool, devils lurk.

Still waters run deep.

11

ГДЕ ЛЮБО́ВЬ, ТАМ И БОГ.

Where love is, God is also.

12

ГЛУ́ПЫЙ ОСУ́ДИТ, А У́МНЫЙ РАССУ́ДИТ.

A fool will condemn, but a wise man will ponder.

Don't rush to judgment.

13

ГОРБА́ТОГО МОГИ́ЛА ИСПРА́ВИТ.

(Only) the grave will straighten a hunchback.

Don't expect a leopard to change its spots.

14

ДАЙ СЕ́РДЦУ ВО́ЛЮ, ЗАВЕДЁТ В НЕВО́ЛЮ.

Give free rein to your heart and it will lead to loss of freedom.

The advantage of the emotions is that they lead us astray. - Wilde

15

ДЕРЖИ́ ЯЗЫ́К ЗА ЗУБА́МИ.

Keep your tongue behind your teeth.

Hold your tongue.

16

ДОЛГ ПЛАТЕЖО́М КРА́СЕН.

A debt is fine in the repayment.

One good turn deserves another.

17

ДРУ́ЖБА – ДРУ́ЖБОЙ, А СЛУ́ЖБА – СЛУ́ЖБОЙ.

Friendship is friendship, but duty is duty.

Business and friendship don't mix.

18

ДУРА́К ДУРАКА́ ВИ́ДИТ ИЗДАЛЕКА́.

A fool sees a fool from afar.

It takes one to know one.

19

ДУРАКА́М ЗАКО́Н НЕ ПИ́САН.

The law isn't written for fools.

There's no telling what a fool will do.

20

**ЖЕНУ́ ВЫБИРА́Й НЕ ГЛАЗА́МИ,
А УША́МИ.**

Choose a wife by your ears rather than your eyes.

Her voice was ever soft, gentle, and low; an excellent thing in woman. – Shakespeare

21

ЖИ́ЗНЬ ПРОЖИ́ТЬ - НЕ ПО́ЛЕ ПЕРЕЙТИ́.

To live one's life is not like crossing a field.

Life is not a bowl of cherries.

22

ЗА ДВУМЯ́ ЗА́ЙЦАМИ ПОГО́НИШЬСЯ, НИ ОДНОГО́ НЕ ПОЙМА́ЕШЬ.

If you chase after two hares, you won't catch even one.

A bird in the hand is worth two in the bush.

23

ЗЕМЛЯ́ ЕСИ́ И В ЗЕ́МЛЮ ОТЫ́ДЕШИ.

You are of the earth and unto the earth you shall return.

Earth to earth, ashes to ashes.

24

ИЗ ОГНЯ́, ДА В ПО́ЛЫМЯ.

Out of the fire, into the flame.

Out of the frying pan, into the fire.

25

КАК АУ́КНЕТСЯ, ТАК И ОТКЛИ́КНЕТСЯ.

As the call, so the echo.

As you sow, so shall you reap.

26

КА́ШУ МА́СЛОМ НЕ ИСПО́РТИШЬ.

You won't spoil the porridge with butter.

You can never have too much of a good thing.

27

КОРÓВА РОДИ́Т, А У БЫКÁ ХВÓСТ БОЛИ́Т.

The cow is giving birth, but the bull's tail hurts.

Don't be a crybaby.

28

КТО ЗА ПРА́ВДУ ГОРО́Й, ТОТ И́СТЫЙ ГЕРО́Й.

Whoever is for the truth with all his might
is a true hero.

Without truth there can be no virtue.

29

КТО НУЖДЫ́ НЕ ВИДА́Л, НЕ ЗНА́ЕТ И СЧА́СТЬЯ.

Anyone who has not known need has not known happiness.

One does not appreciate happiness unless one has known sorrow.

30

КТО СПЕШИ́Т, ТОТ ЛЮДЕ́Й НАСМЕШИ́Т.

People who hurry make a laughing stock of themselves.

Haste makes waste.

31

**КТО СТА́РОЕ ВСПОМЯ́НЕТ,
ТОМУ́ ГЛАЗА́ ВОН.**

One who dwells on the past, should have his eyes plucked out.

Let bygones be bygones.

32

ЛБОМ СТЕ́НУ НЕ ПРОШИБЁШЬ.

You won't smash through a wall with your forehead.

There's no use beating your head against a brick wall.

33

ЛУ́ЧШЕ ХЛЕБ С ВОДО́Ю, ЧЕМ ПИРО́Г С БЕДО́Ю.

Bread with water is better than a pie with trouble.

It's better to be poor but at peace than rich and in trouble.

34

ЛЮ́БИШЬ КАТА́ТЬСЯ, ЛЮБИ́ И СА́НОЧКИ ВОЗИ́ТЬ.

If you like to ride, then like pulling the sled.

He who would call the tune, must pay the piper.

35

ЛЮБО́ВЬ ЗЛА, ПОЛЮ́БИШЬ И КОЗЛА́.

Love is wicked; you can even fall in love with a goat.

Love is blind.

36

МЕ́НЬШЕ ГОВОРИ́, БО́ЛЬШЕ ДЕ́ЛАЙ.

Say less but do more.

Actions speak louder than words.

37

МОЛЧА́НИЕ - ЗНАК СОГЛА́СИЯ.

Silence is a sign of agreement.

Silence gives consent.

38

МЯ́ГКО СТЕ́ЛЕТ, ДА ЖЁСТКО СПАТЬ.

[The bed's] softly made, but it's hard to sleep.

An iron fist in a velvet glove.

39

НА БÓГА НАДÉЙСЯ, А САМ НЕ ПЛОШÁЙ.

Put your hope in God, but don't fall short yourself.

Trust in God, but keep your powder dry.

40

НА ВКУС И ЦВЕТ ТОВА́РИЩА НЕТ.

When it comes to taste and color, there is no kindred spirit.

Each to his own taste.

41

НА ВÓРЕ ШÁПКА ГОРИ́Т.

On a thief the cap is ablaze.

A wrongdoer stands out like a sore thumb.

42

НА ЧУЖО́Й КАРАВА́Й РОТ НЕ РАЗЕВА́Й.

Don't gape at someone else's bread.

Thrust not your feet under another man's table.

43

НА ЧУЖУ́Ю РАБО́ТУ ГЛЯ́ДЯ СЫТ НЕ БУ́ДЕШЬ.

You won't get full by watching someone else's work.

God helps those who help themselves.

44

НАЗВА́ЛСЯ ГРУ́ЗДЕМ, ПОЛЕЗА́Й В КУ́ЗОВ.

If you call yourself a mushroom, crawl into the basket.

In for a penny, in for a pound.

45

НЕ В СВОЙ СА́НИ НЕ САДИ́СЬ.

Don't sit down in someone else's sled.

Paddle your own canoe.

46

НЕ ВСЁ ЗО́ЛОТО, ЧТО БЛЕСТИ́Т.

Not everything that glitters is gold.

All that glitters is not gold.

47

НЕ В СИ́ЛЕ БОГ, А В ПРА́ВДЕ.

God is found not in power, but in truth.

48

НЕ В ДЕНЬГА́Х СЧА́СТЬЕ.

Money is not what brings happiness.

Money can't buy happiness.

49

НЕ ЗНА́Я БРО́ДУ, НЕ СУ́ЙСЯ В ВО́ДУ.

If you don't know the ford, don't get into the water.

Look before you leap.

50

НЕ ИМЕ́Й СТО РУБЛЕ́Й, А ИМЕ́Й СТО ДРУЗЕ́Й.

Don't have 100 rubles – have 100 friends.

Where your friends are, there too are your riches.

51

НЕ КРАСНА́ ИЗБА́ УГЛА́МИ, А КРАСНА́ ПИРОГА́МИ.

A cottage is beautiful not for its corners, but for its pies.

The glory of the house is hospitality.

52

НЕ МЕЧИ́ БИ́СЕР ПЕРЕД СВИ́НЬЯМИ.

Don’t cast pearls before swine.

53

НЕ ОТВЕ́ДАВ ГО́РЬКОГО, НЕ УЗНА́ЕШЬ СЛА́ДКОГО.

Without having tasted the bitter, you will not know the sweet.

You have to take the bitter with the sweet.

54

НЕ ПЛЮЙ В КОЛО́ДЕЦ, ПРИГОДИ́ТСЯ ВОДЫ́ НАПИ́ТЬСЯ.

Don't spit into the well; you may need to drink from it one day.

Don't foul the well, you may need its waters.

55

НЕ РУБИ́ СУК, НА КОТО́РОМ СИДИ́ШЬ.

Don't chop the branch on which you're sitting.

Don't saw the branch you're sitting on.

56

НЕТ РО́ЗЫ БЕЗ ШИПО́В.

There is no rose without thorns.

57

НЕТ ХУ́ДА БЕЗ ДОБРА́.

There's nothing bad without some good.

Every cloud has a silver lining.

58

НЕ́ЧЕГО НА ЗЕ́РКАЛО ПЕНЯ́ТЬ, КО́ЛИ РО́ЖА КРИВА́.

Don’t blame the mirror if your mug is crooked.

Don’t shoot the messenger.

59

ОДИ́Н В ПО́ЛЕ НЕ ВО́ИН.

One man in the field is not a warrior.

There is safety in numbers.

60

ОТ ДОБРА́ ДОБРА́ НЕ И́ЩУТ.

Don't look for good from good.

Leave well enough alone.

61

ОТ СУДЬБЫ́ НЕ УЙДЁШЬ.

You won't escape from fate.

What will be, will be.

62

ПОДНЯ́ВШИЙ МЕЧ ПОГИ́БНЕТ ОТ МЕЧА́.

He who has brandished the sword, shall perish by the sword.

He who lives by the sword, shall die by the sword.

63

ПО ОДЁЖКЕ ВСТРЕЧА́ЮТ - ПО УМУ́ ПРОВОЖА́ЮТ.

People meet judging (you) by your clothes; they part judging (you) by your intelligence.

Charm strikes the sight, but merit wins the soul. – Pope

64

ПРА́ВДА ГЛАЗА́ КО́ЛЕТ.

Truth stabs the eyes.

The truth hurts.

65

ПУ́ГАНАЯ ВОРО́НА И КУСТА́ БОИ́ТСЯ.

A frightened crow fears even a bush.

A burnt child fears the fire.

66

ПЬЯ́НОМУ - МО́РЕ ПО КОЛЕ́НО.

To the drunkard, the sea is knee-deep.

Fools rush in where angels fear to tread. - Pope

67

РЫБА́К РЫБАКА́ ВИ́ДИТ ИЗДАЛЕКА́.

A fisherman recognizes another fisherman from afar.

Birds of a feather flock together.

68

С ВОЛКА́МИ ЖИТЬ, ПО ВО́ЛЧЬИ ВЫТЬ.

He who lives with wolves, will howl like a wolf.

If you lie down with dogs, you'll get up with fleas.

69

С КЕМ ПОВЕДЁШЬСЯ, ОТ ТОГÓ И НАБЕРЁШЬСЯ.

[The person] with whom you hang around, from him will you learn.

A man is known by the company he keeps.

70

С МИ́ЛЫМ РАЙ И В ШАЛАШЕ́.

With a loved one, it's paradise even in a lean-to.

A cottage is a castle for those in love

71

С МИ́РУ ПО НИ́ТКЕ - ГО́ЛОМУ РУБА́ШКА.

If everyone gives a thread, the naked man will get a shirt.

Every little bit helps.

72

СЕДИНА́ В БО́РОДУ, А БЕС В РЕБРО́.

Gray in the beard, but a devil in the rib.

There is no fool like an old fool.

73

СÉМЕРО ОДНОГÓ НЕ ЖДУ́Т.

Seven don't wait for one.

The majority rules.

74

СЛЕЗА́МИ ГО́РЮ НЕ ПОМО́ЖЕШЬ.

Tears will not relieve sorrow.

Crying won't get you anywhere.

75

СЛО́ВО НЕ ВОРОБЕ́Й - ВЫ́ЛЕТИТ, НЕ ПОЙМА́ЕШЬ.

A word is not a sparrow – if it flies away, you won't catch it.

Words have wings and cannot be recalled.

76

СЛУ́ХОМ ЗЕМЛЯ́ ПО́ЛНИТСЯ.

The earth is filled with rumors.

A little bird told me.

СНЯ́ВШИ ГО́ЛОВУ, ПО ВОЛОСА́М НЕ ПЛА́ЧУТ.

Having lopped off the head, don't shed tears over the hair.

It's no use crying over spilt milk.

78

СОЛОВЬЯ́ БА́СНЯМИ НЕ КО́РМЯТ.

Nightingales are not fed with fables.

Fine words butter no parsnips.

79

СТА́РОСТЬ - НЕ РА́ДОСТЬ.

Old age is no joy.

80

СТА́РЫЙ ДРУГ ЛУ́ЧШЕ НО́ВЫХ ДВУХ.

An old friend is better than two new ones.

Old friends are best.

81

ТВОИ́МИ УСТА́МИ МЁД БЫ ПИТЬ.

I would drink honey from your lips.

May your word come true.

82

ТИ́ШЕ Е́ДЕШЬ, ДА́ЛЬШЕ БУ́ДЕШЬ.

If you travel more slowly, you will get farther.

Slow and steady win the race.

83

У КОГО́ ЧТО БОЛИ́Т, ТОТ О ТОМ И ГОВОРИ́Т.

When someone has pain, he talks about nothing else.

He has a bee in his bonnet.

84

У СТРА́ХА ГЛАЗА́ ВЕЛИКИ́.

Fear has big eyes.

Don't make a mountain out of a molehill.

85

УТОПА́ЮЩИЙ И ЗА СОЛО́МИНКУ ХВАТА́ЕТСЯ.

A drowning man clutches at a straw.

Any port in a storm.

86

У́ТРО ВЕ́ЧЕРА МУДРЕНЕ́Е.

Morning is wiser than evening.

The early bird catches the worm.

87

УЧЕ́НЬЕ - СВЕТ, А НЕУЧЕ́НЬЕ - ТЬМА́.

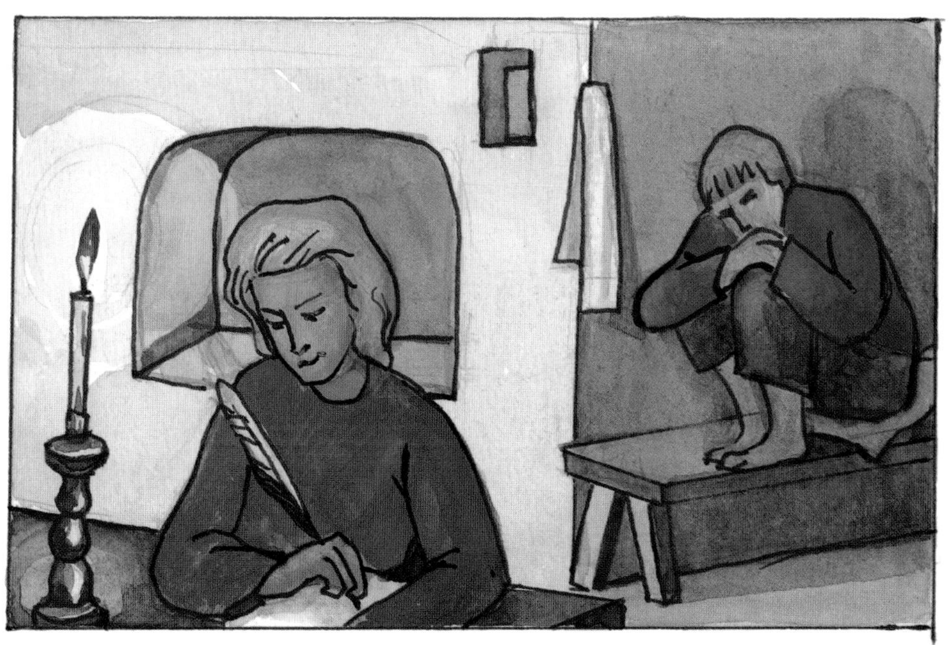

Learning is light; ignorance is darkness.

88

ХУДО́Й МИР ЛУ́ЧШЕ ДО́БРОЙ ССО́РЫ.

A bad peace is better than a good quarrel.

Better a bad peace than a good fight.

89

ХУ́ДО ТОМУ́, КТО ДОБРА́ НЕ ТВОРИ́Т НИКОМУ́.

A pox on him who fails to do good unto others.

Do unto others as you would have them do unto you.

90

ЧЕМ ДА́ЛЬШЕ В ЛЕС, ТЕМ БО́ЛЬШЕ ДРОВ.

The farther you go into the forest,
the more firewood (you find).

91

ЧТО ИМЕ́ЕМ, НЕ ХРАНИ́М, ПОТЕРЯ́ВШИ – ПЛА́ЧЕМ.

We don't take care of what we have, and having lost it we weep.

You never miss the water until the well runs dry.

92

ЧТО НАПИ́САНО ПЕРО́М, НЕ ВЫ́РУБИШЬ И ТОПОРО́М.

What's been written with a pen, can't be chopped out even with an axe.

The pen is mightier than the sword.

93

ЧТО ПОСЕ́ЕШЬ, ТО И ПОЖНЁШЬ.

As you sow, so shall you reap.

94

ЧТО С ГУ́СЯ ВОДА́.

Like water off a goose.

Like water off a duck's back.

95

ЧТО У ТРЕ́ЗВОГО НА УМЕ́, ТО У ПЬЯ́НОГО НА ЯЗЫКЕ́.

What the sober man has on his mind, the drunkard has on his tongue.

In vino veritas.

96

ЧУЖА́Я ДУША́ - ПОТЁМКИ.

Someone else's soul is darkness.

The human soul is a mystery.

97

ЧУЖИ́М НЕ НАЖИВЁШЬСЯ.

You shouldn't profit at someone else's expense.

98

ЭТО ТО́ЛЬКО ЦВЕТО́ЧКИ, А Я́ГОДКИ ЕЩЁ ВПЕРЕДИ́.

These are just the blossoms – the berries are yet to come.

The worst is yet to come.

99

Я́БЛОКО ОТ Я́БЛОНИ НЕДАЛЕКО́ ПА́ДАЕТ.

The apple doesn't fall far from the apple tree.

He's a chip off the old block.
Like father, like son

100

Я́ЙЦА КУ́РИЦУ НЕ У́ЧАТ.

Eggs don't teach the hen.

Don't teach your grandmother to suck eggs.

Donors

THE FOLLOWING FORMER STUDENTS, FRIENDS AND ADMIRERS OF PROFESSOR NADEZHDA TIMOFEEVNA KOROTON ARE GRATEFULLY ACKNOWLEDGED FOR THEIR FINANCIAL CONTRIBUTIONS THAT MADE THIS PUBLICATION POSSIBLE.

Donald L. Alexander '56
Bernard C. Baehler '58
John E. Baldwin, PhD '59
Richard S. Borland, JD '59
Hugh M. Brady '55
Nathan Burkan, Jr. JD '53
Michael Butterworth '63
Lucien H. Case '54
William B. Chapin, III '55
Francis J. Chase '55
Kisuk Cheung '53
Aram M. Chorebanian, JD '51
James G. Churchill '52
George W. Cobb '68
Gerald L. Cohen '62
Duane D. Conover '59
William B. Conway '52
Albert T.T. Cook, Jr. '62
J. Terry Corbet '62
James M. Culberson, Jr. '51
Rev. W. Shepley Curtis, Jr. '65
Albert J. Czaja, MD '65
Rev. Richard A. Ellis '52
John U. Farley, PhD '57
Robert G. Fisher, MD
Leonard I. Gochman '53
Harry S. Goldsmith, MD '52
Frederick C. Gray '64
Robert S. Hagen '69
Danforth A. Hall '52
Richard A. Hall '53
George C. Hibben '52
John A. Hoskins '51
John B. Huck '53
Raymond E. Jankowich, MD '52
Colman W. Kraft '53
Malcolm E. Lambing, Jr. '56
Ralph Lindheim '59
Robert O. Linding '58
Caleb Loring, III '66
Weyman I. Lundquist, JD '52
Robert B. MacPhail, Jr. '62
Robert A. Maguire, PhD '51
Leon C. Martel, Jr. PhD '55
Michael J. McConnell '66
Gordon B. Megibow '65
Patrick M. Morris '60
Richard P. Morse '53
William C. Mutterperl '68
Evelyn Steffanson Nef
Howard N. Newman '56
Thomas M. Nichols, MD '56
George T. Nimitz '54
Paul K. Oltman '60
David W. Overton '61
Theodore G. Pantos, MD
Edward E. Parsons, III '53
Emery L. Pierson '53
Vera Koroton Politis
Alan A. Reich '52
Peter B. Reich '53
Robin Robinson, PhD '24
Kenneth A. Rogers '59
Georg Russanow, MD
Angus M. Russell '52
L. Vincent Sawyer, Jr. '59
L. Ronald Scheman '53
Oleg P. Schidlowsky, MD
George F. Sherman, Jr. '52
Igor I. Sikorsky
Michael N. Skaredoff, MD '69
Joseph D. Spound '51

Names continued on next page.

John K. Springer '53
Mark I. Starr, JD '55
Alanson P. Stevens, III '57
David P. Stiff, MD '53
Samuel T. Swansen, JD '59
William M. Todd, III PhD '66
Walter Tumeniuk '54
Vladimir G. Ulitin, PhD
Capt. Arthur K. Walters, Jr. '59
Richard K. Watt, PhD '54
Daniel R. Woodhead '57
Christopher S. Wren '57

Donors in boldface contributed more than $500.

FUTURE DONATIONS FURTHERING THE WORK AND IDEALS AT DARTMOUTH COLLEGE OF PROFESSOR NADEZHDA TIMOFEEVNA KOROTON MAY BE MADE TO THE "NADEZHDA TIMOFEEVNA KOROTON FUND IN RUSSIAN", ESTABLISHED BY RICHARD P. MORSE '53 AND FORWARDED TO THE GIFT RECORDING, DARTMOUTH COLLEGE, FLEET BANK BUILDING, 63 SOUTH MAIN STREET, HANOVER, NH 03755